Advice to the Players

Bruce Bonafede

A Samuel French Acting Edition

SAMUELFRENCH.COM
SAMUELFRENCH-LONDON.CO.UK

Copyright © 1985, 2014 by Bruce Bonafede
All Rights Reserved

ADVICE TO THE PLAYERS is fully protected under the copyright laws of the United States of America, the British Commonwealth, including Canada, and all other countries of the Copyright Union. All rights, including professional and amateur stage productions, recitation, lecturing, public reading, motion picture, radio broadcasting, television and the rights of translation into foreign languages are strictly reserved.

ISBN **978-0-573-70198-6**

www.SamuelFrench.com
www.SamuelFrench-London.co.uk

FOR PRODUCTION ENQUIRIES

UNITED STATES AND CANADA
Info@SamuelFrench.com
1-866-598-8449

UNITED KINGDOM AND EUROPE
Theatre@SamuelFrench-London.co.uk
020-7255-4302

Each title is subject to availability from Samuel French, depending upon country of performance. Please be aware that *ADVICE TO THE PLAYERS* may not be licensed by Samuel French in your territory. Professional and amateur producers should contact the nearest Samuel French office or licensing partner to verify availability.

CAUTION: Professional and amateur producers are hereby warned that *ADVICE TO THE PLAYERS* is subject to a licensing fee. Publication of this play(s) does not imply availability for performance. Both amateurs and professionals considering a production are strongly advised to apply to Samuel French before starting rehearsals, advertising, or booking a theatre. A licensing fee must be paid whether the title(s) is presented for charity or gain and whether or not admission is charged. Professional/Stock licensing fees are quoted upon application to Samuel French.

No one shall make any changes in this title(s) for the purpose of production. No part of this book may be reproduced, stored in a retrieval system, or transmitted in any form, by any means, now known or yet to be invented, including mechanical, electronic, photocopying, recording, videotaping, or otherwise, without the prior written permission of the publisher. No one shall upload this title(s), or part of this title(s), to any social media websites.

For all enquiries regarding motion picture, television, and other media rights, please contact Samuel French.

MUSIC USE NOTE

Licensees are solely responsible for obtaining formal written permission from copyright owners to use copyrighted music in the performance of this play and are strongly cautioned to do so. If no such permission is obtained by the licensee, then the licensee must use only original music that the licensee owns and controls. Licensees are solely responsible and liable for all music clearances and shall indemnify the copyright owners of the play(s) and their licensing agent, Samuel French, against any costs, expenses, losses and liabilities arising from the use of music by licensees. Please contact the appropriate music licensing authority in your territory for the rights to any incidental music.

IMPORTANT BILLING AND CREDIT REQUIREMENTS

If you have obtained performance rights to this title, please refer to your licensing agreement for important billing and credit requirements.

ADVICE TO THE PLAYERS was first produced by the Philadelphia Festival Theatre for New Plays at the Harold Prince Theater of the Annenberg Center in April 1986. The performance was directed by David Rotenberg, with sets by Eric Schaeffer, costumes by Vicky Esposito and lighting by Curt Senie. The cast was as follows:

OLIVER MANZI	Rozwill Young
ROBERT OBOSA	Lou Ferguson
JOHN TYLER	William Wise
TONY JONES	Peter Wray
RANDALL MOORE	Warren Keith
EMILY NGOME	Lorey Hayes

An earlier version of ***ADVICE TO THE PLAYERS*** was first produced at Actors Theater of Louisville's "Shorts" Festival in November 1984. The performance was directed by Larry Deckel, with sets by Paul Owen, costumes by Marcia Dixcy, lighting by Jeff Hill, and sound by James M. Bay. The Stage Manager was Bob Hornung. The cast was as follows:

OLIVER MANZI	Joe Morton
ROBERT OBOSA	Delroy Lindo
JOHN TYLER	Michael Kevin
TONY JONES	Steven Rankin
RANDALL MOORE	Lanny Flaherty
EMILY NGOME	Cheryl Lynn Bruce

This play was inspired by an actual incident, but is not intended as a portrayal of that incident. All the characters, organizations and events are either products of the author's imagination or are used fictitiously.

The author wishes to thank Grove Press, Inc., for permission to use material from *Waiting for Godot* by Samuel Beckett in this play.

CHARACTERS

OLIVER MANZI – Male, black, South African
ROBERT OBOSA – Male, black, South African
JOHN TYLER – Male, white, American
TONY JONES – Male, white, American
RANDALL MOORE – Male, white, American
EMILY NGOME – Female, black, South African

SETTING

A theatre in the United States.

A banner above the stage, high up, proclaims our presence at the 1981 International Theatre Festival. This remains in place throughout the play.

A playing area has been created center stage by means of either a low platform or painted floor. Upstage of it a flat back curtain of the same width, capable of being drawn open; when so, revealing either the back wall or an empty space – that is to say, nothing of interest.

The playing area is set for a production of *Waiting for Godot*. There is a tree, with four or five leaves. There is a low mound. There is nothing else. It is a stark landscape. It is meant to represent a South African landscape. Both the platform and the back curtain are the color of the veldt.

On both sides of the playing area the stage is in a state of obvious undress. Signs of preparation everywhere. The floor is unswept. All about are ladders, scrap lumber, tools, trash barrels, paint brushes and cans. Amid all this is a folding table with a few metal chairs around it. This too is covered with rehearsal debris: bits of food and wrappers, paper cups of coffee, butt cans, an over-filled ashtray, copies of scripts and highlighters.

Somewhere off the playing area is a road box with the words Cape Town Theatre Co. stenciled across it.

TIME
1981

The play is to be performed without intermission.

"To be a committed political animal today is to care for something more than truth, to involve oneself in compromise for the sake of the well-being and progress of man. But if politics is the art of the possible, art is the politics of the impossible... The artist lives in compromised reality, but he lives in another world as well..."

– Robert Brustein

*(**AT RISE:** Pale moonlight rises on the playing area. The rest of the stage remains in darkness. **TYLER** sits at the table, unseen. **OLIVER MANZI (ESTRAGON)** and **ROBERT OBOSA (VLADIMIR)** are in the playing area, near the tree, in costume. **OLIVER**'s boots are down center. His baggy trousers are down around his ankles. He holds out a long piece of cord. **ROBERT** looks on.)*

OLIVER. *(as* **ESTRAGON***)* Didi.

ROBERT. *(as* **VLADIMIR***)* Yes.

OLIVER. *(as* **ESTRAGON***)* I can't go on like this.

ROBERT. *(as* **VLADIMIR***)* That's what you think.

OLIVER. *(as* **ESTRAGON***)* If we parted? That might be better for us.

ROBERT. *(as* **VLADIMIR***)* We'll hang ourselves tomorrow. *(Pause)* Unless Godot comes.

OLIVER. *(as* **ESTRAGON***)* And if he comes?

ROBERT. *(as* **VLADIMIR***)* We'll be saved.

(He takes off his hat, peers inside it, feels about inside it, shakes it, knocks on the crown, puts it on again.)

OLIVER. *(as* **ESTRAGON***)* Well? Shall we go?

ROBERT. *(as* **VLADIMIR***)* Pull on your trousers.

OLIVER. *(as* **ESTRAGON***)* What?

ROBERT. *(as* **VLADIMIR***)* Pull on your trousers.

OLIVER. *(as* **ESTRAGON***)* You want me to pull off my trousers?

ROBERT *(as* **VLADIMIR***)* Pull ON your trousers.

OLIVER. *(as* **ESTRAGON***, realizing that his trousers are down.)* True.

(He pulls up his trousers.)

ROBERT. *(as* **VLADIMIR***)* Well? Shall we go?

OLIVER *(as* **ESTRAGON***)* Yes, let's go.

(They do not move.)

TYLER. *(his voice comes from the darkness)* They do not move.

(The light on the playing area begins to fade out. Suddenly something goes wrong, and **TYLER***, at the table, finds himself brightly illuminated.)*

TYLER. *(cont.)* What the...?! Hey! In the booth!

(He leaps to his feet, looks in the direction of the theatre's lighting booth, points to the spotlight that has him illuminated. It flicks off. The fade-out continues. During this:)

TYLER. *(cont.)* Okay – okay – much better. *(At black:)* Good!

(The work lights come on.)

TYLER. *(cont.)* Okay, take a break!

(He turns to the actors.)

That was fantastic.

*(***OLIVER** *does not move. He remains in position, staring off, holding up his trousers.* **ROBERT** *takes off his hat, bows slightly to* **TYLER***.)*

ROBERT. Thank you.

TYLER. Thank you. Thank you both. It's going to be great.

ROBERT. You think so?

TYLER. Are you kidding? Of course. *(Pause)* Why, don't you?

ROBERT. I'll be better tonight – when we open.

TYLER. I don't see how.

*(***ROBERT** *moves to the table, begins to look something up in a script.* **TYLER** *glances at* **OLIVER***, but doesn't seem to realize he has not moved.)*

TYLER. *(cont.)* I mean it. Do you have any idea how many times I've seen *Waiting for Godot*?

ROBERT. No.

TYLER. *(laughs)* Neither do I, to tell you the truth. Probably a dozen productions. I've directed it – let's see – this'll be the fourth time.

ROBERT. The fourth? Really?

TYLER. Well, if you count once in college. But I've never seen it done the way you two do it.

ROBERT. *(laughs)* Is that good?

TYLER. What? Oh. *(Laughs)* I mean it. It's almost as though the thing was written for you.

ROBERT. Please, I am not that old.

(He has found what he wanted, puts the script down on the table.)

TYLER. Oh, I know. What I mean – I can see why you've done so well with the play – like in London.

ROBERT. Ah, London!

(He moves to the road box, puts in his hat, takes out a towel, wipes his hands, hangs it around his neck.)

TYLER. Yes – why it was such a smash for you there.

ROBERT. They seemed to like us.

TYLER. *Like* you? Robert, you don't need to be so modest. You got a lot of acclaim – don't downplay it. *I* haven't. I've put it into all our advertising for the festival – "London triumph", "World tour" –

ROBERT. World?

TYLER. From Africa to England *and* America? I'd say that qualifies. *(Pause)* I didn't think you'd mind.

ROBERT. *(smiles)* No, no.

TYLER. You're giving us a great opening this year.

ROBERT. We hope so.

TYLER. Oh, you are, believe me. Having you here is a real coup for us.

ROBERT. For us, too.

TYLER. You must be looking forward to going on to New York.

ROBERT. Yes, but we are happy to be *here*. Our first performance in America – something very special for us.

TYLER. You mean that?

ROBERT. Of course.

TYLER. I just wish we had you for a regular run. A week is so short.

ROBERT. It is short.

TYLER. Maybe, if you like working here, you'll think about coming back next year – ?

ROBERT. *(smiles)* And do *Godot* again?

TYLER. Not necessarily. You could do whatever you choose.

ROBERT. You mean that?

TYLER. Yes, I do. Assuming we can afford it.

*(**ROBERT** laughs. **TONY** comes onstage.)*

TONY. *(to **TYLER**)* If you need me for anything, I'll be up front.

(He picks up the tree, begins to carry it off.)

TYLER. Okay, Tony. Get some lunch if you want. We probably won't do any more 'til the others get here.

TONY. *(to **ROBERT**)* Sorry about the fade. We'll get it right, don't worry.

ROBERT. I'm sure. Thank you.

*(As **TONY** exits with the tree, he notices **OLIVER** still standing there, does a double-take, keeps walking.)*

ROBERT. *(cont.)* "Do whatever we choose" – I like the sound of that.

TYLER. I mean it. That'd be fine with me. And like I said, the only restriction would be what we can handle in our budget – as always.

ROBERT. I understand. We have our theatre, too.

TYLER. I'm not looking for a commitment now. Just think about it. We can talk more later.

ROBERT. All right.

TYLER. I want you to feel completely comfortable with your experience here. I hope you do.

ROBERT. Yes

TYLER. Good.

ROBERT. You have a fine group of people working with you.

TYLER. They're all thrilled to be working with *you.* So am I, you know, though I have to admit I don't feel like I've done much work.

ROBERT. That's not true.

TYLER. As a director, I mean.

ROBERT. You've given us a lot of freedom, and we appreciate it.

TYLER. Well, I want your vision of the play here, not mine. As long as it's good for the show, I don't mind being a figurehead.

ROBERT. That's not what you have been.

TYLER. Well, toward you I have, but I meant to be.

ROBERT. Not toward your people, though.

TYLER. I hope that hasn't made you uncomfortable.

ROBERT. What?

TYLER. Having to use our people in the other roles.

ROBERT. No, no. They are very good.

TYLER. It's too bad the rest of your company couldn't come.

ROBERT. They couldn't come to London either.

TYLER. That must've been hard on you.

ROBERT. Harder on them, I think. They were very disappointed.

TYLER. I can imagine. Why did they do it?

ROBERT. Our people?

TYLER. Your government.

ROBERT. Oh. Why? They have done this sort of thing to us for years. We live in a beautiful land where there is much ugliness.

TYLER. They interfere with your plans?

ROBERT. All the time. We're accustomed to such – small punishments.

TYLER. It must be tough to deal with.

ROBERT. *(laughs)* Yes, well, better a small punishment than one of their big ones.

TYLER. I suppose –

ROBERT. Oh, yes – believe me. But the small ones – the small ones are hard, too – because they never stop. They are always putting restrictions on us of one kind or another – trying to intimidate us, discourage us – get us to give up, or at least stay home and be good – keep quiet. We have never been. We make a lot of noise – and we don't let them stop us from coming to America – right, Oliver?

*(He looks around, sees **OLIVER**.)*

What are you doing?

*(**OLIVER** is still standing motionless, staring off, holding up his trousers. He does not look at **ROBERT**.)*

OLIVER. *(stage whisper)* Are you speaking to me?

ROBERT. Yes. Why are you standing there?

OLIVER. Why?

ROBERT. Yes.

OLIVER. Why do you think?

ROBERT. I don't know.

OLIVER. Isn't it obvious?

ROBERT. No.

OLIVER. I'm waiting for Godot.

*(**TYLER** laughs.)*

ROBERT. Oh, you are?

OLIVER. Yes.

ROBERT. But, Oliver – the play is over.

OLIVER. *(pause)* Over?

ROBERT. Yes. Come now – time to return to reality.

OLIVER. *(after a pause)* Shit.

(He tugs up his trousers, ties them with his cord.)

ROBERT. *(To* **TYLER***)* Don't worry. I never let him fool with the play in an actual performance.

TYLER. Oh, I know the routine by now. Are you two ever offstage?

OLIVER. Only when absolutely necessary.

ROBERT. My friend is very childish. He loves to play these little games.

OLIVER. And he loves it when I do.

ROBERT. I?

OLIVER. Yes. You know you do.

(He goes to get his boots)

ROBERT. So?

OLIVER. So – who is more childish?

ROBERT. You are.

OLIVER. I?

ROBERT. Yes.

OLIVER. Not you?

ROBERT. No

OLIVER. Are you certain?

ROBERT. *(they have done this exchange before.)* Nothing is certain.

OLIVER. Nothing is certain?

ROBERT. No

OLIVER. That's terrible. *(Pause)* Are you certain?

ROBERT. Yes.

OLIVER. Ah – that's reassuring.

(He picks up his boots, moves toward **ROBERT***, speaking to* **TYLER.***)*

I am fortunate to have the great Robert Obosa to give me philosophical guidance. He is my intellectual superior, and I take every opportunity to demonstrate the high esteem I hold him in.

*(He thrusts his boots in **ROBERT**'s face.)*

Here, have a lick.

ROBERT. *(recoils)* Stop that! Behave yourself!

OLIVER. *(shrugs)* Though sometimes he doesn't appreciate the gesture.

TYLER. *(laughs)* I can't imagine why not.

ROBERT. Maybe because you are so crude about it.

OLIVER. I am never crude. *(To **TYLER**)* I'm not.

(He takes a paper cup from the rehearsal table, takes a mouthful, spits it violently onto the floor.)

This coffee is colder than those whores we had in Berlin!

ROBERT. Whores? *(To **TYLER**)* You see? *(To **OLIVER**)* Besides, we were never in Berlin.

OLIVER. *(to **TYLER**)* That's what I meant.

TYLER. I'm sorry – it's been out here awhile. There should be some hot in my office.

OLIVER. *(grandly)* I hope so. I don't know how I can be expected to work under these conditions!

ROBERT. He doesn't mean that.

TYLER. *(smiles)* Oh, I know.

OLIVER. I most certainly do. I cannot continue to rehearse if my tongue is frozen.

ROBERT. Oh, I don't know –

OLIVER. *(says the line an instant before him.)* It might help.

ROBERT. – it might – How did you know I was going to say that?

OLIVER. *(to **TYLER**)* I may be childish, but my friend here is very predictable.

ROBERT. Oh, am I?

OLIVER. Yes.

(He begins pulling on his boots.)

ROBERT. Well, I suppose anyone would be – after nine years.

OLIVER. That's true.

ROBERT. You agree?

OLIVER. Yes.

ROBERT. With me?

OLIVER. Even you can't be wrong about everything.

*(***ROBERT** *begins to threaten* **OLIVER** *with the towel, thinks better of it, turns to* **TYLER.***)*

ROBERT. So, what's the plan for today, Mr. Tyler?

TYLER. Please, I told you – it's John.

OLIVER. The plan for today is "John."

ROBERT. Be quiet. *(To* **TYLER***)* John.

TYLER. Well, let's see – I gave everyone else a one-thirty call.

OLIVER. *(excited)* For dress rehearsal?

TYLER. Yes. We'll start at two.

OLIVER. And we go on tonight at eight?

TYLER. That's right.

OLIVER. And the audience? You think we'll have a good crowd?

TYLER. I'm sure. We're sold out for every performance.

ROBERT. He told us that yesterday.

OLIVER. I know – I just like hearing it again.

ROBERT. You'll probably be in the lobby beforehand, offering to autograph programs.

OLIVER. *(indignantly)* I have never done that. *(To* **TYLER***)* Though it isn't a bad idea.

ROBERT. Oliver –

*(***TONY** *enters from the back of the house. He stops before reaching the stage.)*

TONY. John?

TYLER. Yes?

TONY. Sorry to interrupt.

OLIVER. *(quickly)* That's okay.

TYLER. That's – okay.

*(He glances at **OLIVER**, who smiles back.)*

TONY. There's a man out front who wants to see you.

TYLER. Now? Who is it?

TONY. I don't know. He said his name is Moore.

TYLER. I don't think I know him. *(To **ROBERT** and **OLIVER**)* Were you expecting anybody?

OLIVER. Only vast crowds of admirers.

TYLER. Did he say what he wants?

TONY. No. He's wearing a suit.

OLIVER. *(jumps up, terrified)* Don't let him in!

TYLER. *(laughs)* I probably shouldn't. *(To **ROBERT**)* Do you mind?

ROBERT. No, not at all.

TYLER. I'll get rid of him. Okay, Tony.

*(**TONY** exits as he came in.)*

ROBERT. We'll leave you to your business. How long before your people arrive?

TYLER. A little over an hour.

ROBERT. We have some time, then.

TYLER. Yes.

OLIVER. Enough for a round of golf at the country club?

TYLER. *(smiles)* I think so.

OLIVER. Followed by cocktails on the veranda – and maybe a quick one with the governor's wife?

TYLER. *(laughs)* It would have to be quick.

OLIVER. *(ruefully)* Oh, it would be.

ROBERT. I was thinking more of a few minutes' rest.

OLIVER. Rest?

ROBERT. Something we both need.

TYLER. That's probably a better idea.

ROBERT. May we use your office, John?

TYLER. Please.

ROBERT. Thank you. Come along, Oliver.

OLIVER. But, Robert –

ROBERT. We'll get you some hot coffee.

OLIVER. Who wants coffee? We're having cocktails on the veranda!

ROBERT. No. We are not. You are fantasizing again.

OLIVER. I am?

ROBERT. Yes.

OLIVER. We're not going to play golf?

ROBERT. No.

OLIVER. What about the governor's wife?

ROBERT. What about her?

OLIVER. Won't she be disappointed if we don't at least put in an appearance?

ROBERT. Oliver, you made her up – she doesn't exist.

OLIVER. She doesn't?

ROBERT. No.

OLIVER. *(trying to start their joke again)* Are you certain?

ROBERT. *(won't play along this time)* Yes.

OLIVER. Well, there's no point in going, then, is there?

ROBERT. No.

OLIVER. Still, I think we should call. It's only polite to let her know that we're not coming –

*(***ROBERT**, *threatening* **OLIVER** *with the towel, chases him offstage. They exit.* **TYLER** *is at the table. He calls toward the lighting booth.)*

TYLER. Hello, in the booth. Let's run that fade again. I want to see the final lighting cue.

(Blackout.)

No, not the final one – the next one.

(The house lights come up.)

What is this? *(He realizes.)* No, not *that* next one – go back.

(Blackout. Pause.)

One more, please.

(Lights change to pale moonlight on the playing area, as at the end of the Waiting for Godot *sequence.)*

That's it – hold it right there.

(**TYLER**, *at the table, can no longer be seen.* **RANDALL MOORE** *enters from the back of the house.)*

MOORE. *(calls)* Mr. Tyler?

TYLER. Yes?

MOORE. I'm Randall Moore. Pleased to meet you, at last.

(He begins to make his way, in the dark, down the aisle to the stage.)

TYLER. Hi.

MOORE. I appreciate this opportunity to talk with you personally. I find that face-to-face discussions are often the only way to settle situations of this kind.

TYLER. What kind?

MOORE. I'm sure you find that to be true too. Even seemingly irreconcilable positions can be resolved if the sides in opposition will simply sit down and try to communicate with each other.

(He is at the stage, looking for **TYLER**.*)*

TYLER. I don't know what you're talking about.

MOORE. I'm talking about progress – making progress out of adversarial situations.

TYLER. Why?

MOORE. Why what?

TYLER. What adversarial situation?

MOORE. Ours, of course.

TYLER. Ours?

MOORE. Yes.

TYLER. *(calls)* Hello in the booth. Give me the works.

(The moonlight on the playing area disappears and the work lights come on. They are bright enough to disorient **MOORE.** *)*

Who are you?

MOORE. I told you. I assume you remember me. *(Pause)* You don't. Well, I have to admit I didn't expect that.

TYLER. I'm sorry.

MOORE. We spoke a few weeks ago?

TYLER. We met?

MOORE. No. On the phone.

TYLER. Oh.

MOORE. Three, I think – about that.

TYLER. About what?

MOORE. About three weeks.

TYLER. No, I mean what did you call about?

MOORE. Oh. Our request. The coalition's request.

TYLER. The coalition?

MOORE. The Coalition of the Liberation of the South African People. I'm here as their representative.

TYLER. *(realizing)* I see.

MOORE. You remember?

TYLER. Yes. Yes, I do. What are you doing here?

MOORE. I'm here to talk to you about our request.

TYLER. What – now?

MOORE. Yes.

TYLER. I can't talk to you now. You should've called me.

MOORE. I did call you.

TYLER. You did?

MOORE. Several times. Especially over the last few days. You apparently don't get your messages.

TYLER. Well, not always.

MOORE. I assumed you were willing to meet with me. If you weren't why did you let me in?

TYLER. I didn't realize who you were.

MOORE. I see. Well, we're here now – that's the main thing.

TYLER. No, I'm afraid it's not. You don't understand. We're getting ready to open our festival tonight.

MOORE. I'm aware of that.

TYLER. There are a million things going on – things to take care of.

(He waves his arms to suggest great activity, stops. **MOORE** *looks at him for a long moment.)*

MOORE. You don't seem terribly busy right now.

TYLER. Well, I am, even if I don't seem so at the moment. You just happened to come in during a lull.

(During the following, in order to make himself appear busy, he opens the back curtain, makes a show of inspecting it.)

TYLER. *(cont.)* In a little while this theatre's going to be filled with actors and technicians running around. It's all-consuming. There isn't time to deal with anything else.

MOORE. You'll find it in your interest to make the time.

TYLER. No, don't take that wrong, I mean with *anything* else. It would be the same no matter what this was about.

MOORE. I can appreciate that.

TYLER. We're under a deadline that just can't be ignored.

MOORE. Yes, so are we – the same deadline. This is, unless you've decided to agree with our request.

*(***TYLER*** stops fiddling with the curtain. All he has managed to do, though he does not realize it, is reveal whatever was behind the curtain, which should be the back wall or an empty space – that is to say, nothing of interest. For a moment, under work light, and without the back curtain or the tree, the playing area looks like the rest of the stage – void of all magic.)*

TYLER. No.

(**TONY** *comes back onstage with the tree, from which he has removed the leaves. He goes to set it down on its spot, but* **MOORE** *is in the way.* **TONY** *waits for him to move.*)

TYLER. *(cont.)* Excuse me, please.

(**MOORE** *moves out of the way.* **TONY** *sets down the tree, exits.* **TYLER** *busies himself arranging the position of the tree.*)

MOORE. *(After a pause)* You are still planning to allow Oliver Manzi and Robert Obosa to perform?

TYLER. Allow? No, not allow. We invited them. They're our guest artists. Our preeminent guest artists. I'm sorry if you have a problem with that, but –

MOORE. *We* have a problem with that.

TYLER. Your coalition – I know.

MOORE. You and I, Mr. Tyler.

TYLER. As I told you when you called me – three weeks ago – I just don't see it that way.

MOORE. You intend to ignore our request.

TYLER. No, not *ignore*. I don't think that's fair. I talked to you when you first wanted me to.

MOORE. And that's all I'm asking now.

TYLER. This is different. That was reasonable – this isn't reasonable. You can't come in here on the day we're opening –

MOORE. I had no choice, Mr. Tyler. You forced me into this course of action.

TYLER. I didn't force you to do anything.

MOORE. You didn't agree to what we asked.

TYLER. That doesn't give you the right to come marching in –

MOORE. It gives me the responsibility to pursue the matter.

TYLER. You seemed to understand my position when we spoke on the phone.

MOORE. I understood it, yes.

TYLER. And agreed.

MOORE. I never said that.

TYLER. You led me to believe you did.

MOORE. Then you must have misunderstood me.

TYLER. Well, you should've made that clear then. Maybe we could've settled this at the time.

MOORE. We can still settle it.

TYLER. I don't see how.

MOORE. All I want is an opportunity to show you how doing what we ask will be better for you – and your festival – than not.

TYLER. And all I want is for you to understand there isn't any point. Even if I had the time to go over all this again – which I don't – I don't want to do what you ask. And even if I wanted to, there's no way I could now. Our festival's opening tonight. The tickets for every single performance have been sold. I can't disappoint our audiences.

MOORE. *(dryly)* The show must go on.

TYLER. Something like that – credibility.

MOORE. Under normal circumstances, naturally, I'd understand.

TYLER. We have our responsibilities, too.

MOORE. Unfortunately, these aren't normal circumstances. Whether or not these men are allowed to perform here is a matter of utmost urgency to our organization.

TYLER. And to our festival.

MOORE. I assume you support our goal of a free South Africa. Most Americans do.

TYLER. What's that got to do with anything? That's not the question here.

MOORE. But you do – don't you? I mean personally.

TYLER. Personally, of course, but –

MOORE. There, you see? We've already found some common ground. Now we can try to work our way through to an agreement.

TYLER. No, I've already explained –

MOORE. Yes, I know – the time element.

TYLER. That, and because I simply can't do what you ask.

MOORE. Of course you can.

TYLER. No, I can't.

MOORE. You can't?

TYLER. No.

MOORE. Aren't you the artistic director of this theatre?

TYLER. Yes. So?

MOORE. So – you are in authority, aren't you?

TYLER. Yes.

MOORE. And you're in charge of the festival, as well?

TYLER. Yes.

MOORE. So it was your decision which artists to invite?

TYLER. Ultimately.

MOORE. Then you have the authority to, say, disinvite anyone on the festival program. You can do as we ask, it's simply a question of whether you will or not.

TYLER. Look, I'm not a dictator. I'm answerable to the board of trustees.

MOORE. We're all answerable to someone.

TYLER. Especially, I would imagine, on something like this.

MOORE. Should I meet with the board?

TYLER. Well, you can't.

MOORE. Why not?

TYLER. The members aren't all in one place.

MOORE. Can you call them together?

TYLER. Not on such short notice – no.

MOORE. Why not?

TYLER. It's just not possible.

MOORE. Not possible, or you don't want to?

TYLER. Not possible *and* I don't want to.

MOORE. I'm simply trying to determine who's got the authority around here. You say you don't have it – on the other hand –

TYLER. I never said I didn't have the authority to make the decision. I don't have the right to exercise the authority to make the decision. I can't cancel this production. It would go against everything I believe. Plus, I've made a commitment here, to everyone involved – the actors, technicians, the audiences – I have a responsibility to our people

MOORE. I realize that.

(He takes a printed brochure from his briefcase, reads)

"The International Theatre Festival was conceived as a celebration of theatre, and as a means of bringing artists of diverse national origin to the attention of our city for the betterment of our cultural life." Very admirable.

TYLER. Thanks – I know what it says.

MOORE. Then, as your brochure implies, you realize you also have a responsibility to the community your theatre serves – not to offend that community.

TYLER. We're not offending anybody.

MOORE. You are. Everyone who cares about meaningful reform in South Africa – that's what you're doing by having these two men perform here.

TYLER. Then why has no one contacted us to say so?

MOORE. We have.

TYLER. Mr. Moore – to be frank, you don't exactly represent the community. We've sold thousands of tickets to our festival. I've never even heard of your organization.

MOORE. We are well known.

TYLER. Really?

MOORE. By those who care about promoting international human rights.

*(He moves close to **TYLER**.)*

That's why your cooperation with us will be of such benefit to you. People know what we stand for. Once you've allied yourselves with us, it will earn your theatre – and you – a great deal of respect. Locally – even nationally.

TYLER. You mean it could earn us a great deal of publicity.

MOORE. It might.

TYLER. If we got tied in with you on this.

MOORE. Very possibly.

TYLER. Or is it the publicity you'll get?

MOORE. That is insulting.

TYLER. Why? You seem to think I'll jump at the chance to earn publicity for my theatre. You expect me to believe you don't care about the fact you could earn some for your organization?

MOORE. That is not why we're doing this.

TYLER. If you got us to cancel a production for political purposes it would certainly help make a name for your group.

MOORE. We don't need to make a name, Mr. Tyler

TYLER. Well, I'm glad to hear it. Because you won't be doing it through us. This is a theatre. We're not interested in getting involved with politics.

MOORE. Then you shouldn't be letting members of the Cape Town Theatre Company perform here. You shouldn't be making political statements.

TYLER. We're making an artistic statement, not a political one.

MOORE. You may not mean to be making one, but believe me you are. The implications of what you're doing here are outrageous.

TYLER. What implications?

MOORE. This production is a sign of approval of the South African government.

TYLER. That's nonsense.

MOORE. That's how it will be seen.

TYLER. Why? We're talking about two celebrated actors who've performed practically all over the world.

MOORE. We're aware of their reputations. That has nothing to do with it.

TYLER. I've never heard it suggested their work showed approval of their government – quite the opposite.

MOORE. Your having them here is approval enough.

TYLER. But they're black – do you realize that?

MOORE. Even so – to include them in your festival shows that you are willing to have cultural exchange with South Africa.

TYLER. Not with South Africa, with two actors who happen to be South African.

MOORE. And that is a violation of the boycott. We must maintain the boycott, Mr. Tyler. It's the only way the civilized world has to deal with South Africa.

TYLER. We're not trying to deal with anything. We're doing a play.

MOORE. But you could be doing much more. You have a chance here to make a real contribution.

TYLER. Thank you – we're not interested. That's your priority, not ours. Ours is to give our audiences the best possible productions of the best plays we can.

MOORE. Yes, and why? To be of service to your community. "For the betterment of our cultural life" – ?

TYLER. Yes, partly.

MOORE. And that's what we're offering you – a chance to be of service.

TYLER. Artistic service – not political. The two are entirely separate – they have to be.

MOORE. Why?

TYLER. I don't want to discuss this any further.

MOORE. Let me point out –

TYLER. Please –

MOORE. – outline what we will do for you –

TYLER. – no, please –

MOORE. – in return for your cooperation.

TYLER. You're not listening to me! I can't – I *won't* cancel this production. I won't have these two men become pawns in some political game.

MOORE. We are prepared to –

TYLER. No, no – stop! I don't want to hear anymore. *(Pause)* Look, I'm sorry. I'm sure you think you're doing the right thing, but I don't believe you can help the cause of freedom in South Africa by stifling freedom of expression here in America.

MOORE. That's not what we're doing.

TYLER. It seems like it to me.

MOORE. If you will just listen –

TYLER. You're going to end up victimizing two of the men you profess to be trying to help.

MOORE. We're not stifling anyone's freedom. We're trying to help millions *gain* their freedom – and giving up a single production in a theatre festival seems a very small price to pay!

TYLER. Of course it does, to you – this isn't your life. And you may or may not have a point, if it would somehow lead to what you want. But it won't.

MOORE. We disagree.

TYLER. That's obvious.

MOORE. What happens here will have a major effect on the international situation.

TYLER. Oh, come on. You can't really believe that.

MOORE. Yes, we can, and we do. Mr. Tyler, I have to advise you that if you're unwilling to cooperate, we are prepared to take steps.

TYLER. I thought you were just here to talk.

MOORE. Sometimes one has to stop talking and take action.

TYLER. You knew I couldn't cancel.

MOORE. I was prepared for you to be uncooperative.

TYLER. Then why didn't you just make your threats? Why waste my time?

MOORE. I still hoped to convince you.

TYLER. You had no reason to.

MOORE. Even so –

TYLER. All right. What do you plan to do?

MOORE. We plan to exercise our rights. We intend to protest this production.

TYLER. *(almost laughs)* Protest? Well, I can't stop you from doing that.

MOORE. You stop *us*? It's quite the other way around, Mr. Tyler. We intend to stop this production from taking place.

TYLER. You do?

MOORE. And I might add, if you force us to stop this production, we intend to stop the entire festival.

TYLER. Oh? How?

MOORE. We will eliminate your audience.

TYLER. "Eliminate?" *(Laughs)* You're not going to shoot them, are you?

MOORE. That's very funny – no. We have a demonstration standing by right now ready to move in. We are not the ones playing games here, Mr. Tyler.

(The sound of **OLIVER** *shouting and laughing, and then he and* **ROBERT** *come onstage.* **OLIVER** *is in the lead, carefully carrying a full cup of hot coffee.* **ROBERT** *is trying to stop him.)*

OLIVER. John! John!

ROBERT. Oliver –

OLIVER. No, leave me. John!

ROBERT. Stop this, now. Don't –

OLIVER. *(To* **ROBERT***)* Shhh!

*(***ROBERT** *gives up. To* **TYLER***)*

John!

*(He advances on **TYLER**)*

John John John John John.

*(Puts his arm around **TYLER**.)*

I have to tell you – we were just talking about what a lovely theatre you have.

TYLER. Thanks.

OLIVER. We wish we had a place like this at home. Look at this place!

(He tries to make a sweeping grand gesture with his arms, but can only use one arm as he is trying to hold and not spill the coffee with the other.)

TYLER. Well, I wish you did, too, Oliver.

OLIVER. *(sighs)* Ah, yes, ours is nothing like this. Nothing at all. You've heard of Shakespeare in the park? Well, we have Beckett in the basement. Of course, that's kind of appropriate, isn't it?

ROBERT. Oliver!

OLIVER. Hmmm?

ROBERT. You see?

*(He gestures toward **MOORE**.)*

I told you – we're interrupting.

OLIVER. Oh! I'm sorry.

*(He backs away, begins to follow **ROBERT** off.)*

TYLER. No, wait a minute – I'm glad you're here. I think this is someone you should meet.

MOORE. Mr. Tyler, I'm not interested in meeting anyone.

(He picks up his briefcase.)

TYLER. Not even the two men involved?

MOORE. I came here to talk to you, not them. And if you don't mind I'd like to do that alone.

TYLER. Actually, I do mind. Robert Obosa, Oliver Manzi – this is Mr. Moore.

*(**ROBERT** begins to speak. **OLIVER** stops him, pushes him back, advances on **MOORE**, makes a grand bow.)*

OLIVER. An honor, sir.

*(Bowing, he spills his coffee all over **MOORE**'s briefcase and shoes.)*

Oh, shit!

*(**MOORE** is too stunned to move. **OLIVER** rushes about, hands **TYLER** the empty cup, grabs a cloth from the table, begins wiping off **MOORE**'s briefcase, which **MOORE** is still holding.)*

I'm so sorry. That was so clumsy of me –

MOORE. That's quite all right – please – it's all right –

*(**OLIVER** goes down on his knees and, as **MOORE** attempts to pull away, seizes his foot and begins wiping his shoe. **MOORE** nearly falls down.)*

OLIVER. Let me – I am so sorry –

MOORE. It's all right – please!

*(He finally pulls his foot free of **OLIVER**'s grasp.)*

ROBERT. Oliver!

*(He gestures for **OLIVER** to leave **MOORE** alone. **OLIVER** stands, hands **MOORE** the cloth, makes a face at **ROBERT**, retreats. **MOORE** moves away to dry himself off. **TYLER** is both mortified and trying not to laugh.)*

ROBERT. *(cont.)* What's this about us? *(To **MOORE**)* Do you have something to do with the festival?

*(**MOORE** does not answer.)*

TYLER. Well, in a way. You see, there's a bit of a problem.

ROBERT. With the festival?

TYLER. Actually, with your part in it.

OLIVER. Oh no, we're closing before we've even opened!

*(He rushes to **ROBERT**.)*

Isn't this exciting? It's like being on Broadway!

*(**ROBERT** ignores him.)*

ROBERT. What's the problem, John?

TYLER. We're involved in a protest – a protest against your production.

ROBERT. A protest? Against us? By who?

TYLER. By Mr. Moore.

MOORE. By the organization I represent.

*(**OLIVER** pulls **ROBERT** aside. They deliberately speak loudly enough for **MOORE** to hear them.)*

OLIVER. Robert, do you think he's a Nazi?

ROBERT. Oh, no – I don't think so.

OLIVER. How can you tell?

ROBERT. No uniform – no swastika.

OLIVER. Ah, then he must be from the Ku Klux Klan.

ROBERT. Not necessarily.

OLIVER. No?

ROBERT. He's not wearing a sheet. I've heard they always wear sheets.

OLIVER. Always?

ROBERT. Except in bed.

(They break up laughing.)

MOORE. *(to **TYLER**)* I really don't see the point of this.

(He starts to leave)

TYLER. *(to **ROBERT** and **OLIVER**)* Yes. Please – this is very serious.

*(**ROBERT** gestures that they will behave. **MOORE** stops.)*

He's threatening to try to close down the festival if I don't cancel your production.

ROBERT. You mean you're serious? Why in the world are you protesting our production?

MOORE. Because you're South African.

ROBERT. But we are black.

MOORE. That doesn't matter.

OLIVER. It matters to us.

MOORE. The group I represent is opposed to any contact with South Africa.

OLIVER. So am I.

MOORE. You?

OLIVER. Oh, yes, I get out whenever I can.

ROBERT. You are protesting us only because we are South African?

MOORE. That's right.

ROBERT. If we were not South African, but from another country – say, Zimbabwe – you wouldn't care if we performed here?

MOORE. There's no boycott of Zimbabwe. It's been liberated.

OLIVER. Ah, so in South Africa we have race-prejudice, and in America you have nation-prejudice. What is this group that you represent?

MOORE. The Coalition for the Liberation of the South African People.

ROBERT. *(puzzled)* But you are an American.

MOORE. We're an American organization.

OLIVER. Well, we are South African people. Please liberate us by going away!

MOORE. Not until I have Mr. Tyler's promise to do what we demand.

ROBERT. What has he to do with it?

MOORE. He's the one in authority here.

OLIVER. Oh, I'm not sure I like that. I always have trouble with the authorities.

ROBERT. You support the cause of democracy in South Africa?

MOORE. Obviously.

ROBERT. So do we, obviously. You shouldn't be protesting us.

MOORE. We're not protesting you personally. We have nothing against you performing in South Africa. But we can't allow you to perform here because it would be a violation of the boycott.

TYLER. Don't bother trying to convince him he can't help you by hurting you – he doesn't agree.

MOORE. I've already explained my position on that. I won't go through it again.

OLIVER. Oh, please do. It might be good for a laugh.

MOORE. We're unwilling to let anything happen that might help your government.

OLIVER. That makes it unanimous.

ROBERT. Our government has nothing to do with our being here.

MOORE. Hasn't it?

ROBERT. No. They don't even want us here.

MOORE. They let you come.

ROBERT. Yes, so what? They didn't let the rest of our company come.

MOORE. But they did you – why?

ROBERT. We have performed outside the country before, so we are better known than the others. They were afraid of the reaction in the press if they refused us permission.

MOORE. That isn't why.

ROBERT. It isn't?

MOORE. It's because you're being used as propaganda.

(**ROBERT** *and* **OLIVER** *look at each other.*)

Yes, you are well known, and your government knows that. So they let you travel and perform, as though you're free. When the world sees that, they don't care so much what's done to your people at home. Hasn't that ever occurred to you?

ROBERT. No, that has never occurred to me. Only a rich white American who knows nothing at all about us or our country could think such a thing.

OLIVER. *(to MOORE)* Careful – you're making him angry. You don't want to make him angry.

(MOORE turns away from ROBERT.)

MOORE. Mr. Tyler, are you going to cooperate or not?

ROBERT. You are asking the wrong person. You won't stop us by intimidating Mr. Tyler. If we are thrown out of his theatre, we'll do our performance on the bloody street.

MOORE. *(to TYLER)* Do you or don't you want to save your festival?

ROBERT. How do you propose to stop it?

TYLER. He claims he's got a demonstration outside, waiting to move in.

ROBERT. Is that so? How large a demonstration?

MOORE. *(to ROBERT)* Large enough. *(To TYLER)* Large enough to cause you a lot of problems.

TYLER. Of course, if they do, I'll be forced to call the police.

OLIVER. *(jumps, terrified)* The police?!

TYLER. Yes.

OLIVER. You mean, they're on *our* side?

TYLER. Of course.

OLIVER. *(to ROBERT)* Imagine that.

MOORE. They won't help you. I've dealt with them before.

TYLER. You won't set foot in this theatre.

MOORE. We don't need to. We'll set up a line of demonstrators out front. The police will want to talk us, to convince us to give it up and go home. And we'll talk to them – at great length – to the police and at the same time to every TV news team and newspaper in the city. We will accuse you publicly of promoting exchange with South Africa.

TYLER. Which isn't true.

MOORE. We believe it is.

TYLER. Well, I can talk to the media, too, you know. Tell them our side.

MOORE. Fine. Do that. Defend yourselves. The more publicity, the better. How many members of your audience do you think will want to get caught up in a demonstration just to see a play?

TYLER. Then we'll postpone our opening, and demand the police clear you out.

MOORE. Then we'll be back tomorrow, and the next day and the next until this theatre is empty and stays empty. Can you imagine what a fiasco that will make of your festival? How much money do you estimate you'll lose? And just think what that will do to your reputation in the theatre, Mr. Tyler.

TYLER. I don't know. It's a crazy business. It might help.

OLIVER. *(laughs. To* **MOORE***)* I don't think you've convinced him. Would you like me to try?

MOORE. That's very funny.

OLIVER. I mean it – what do you think?

MOORE. I think you ought to take the whole situation more seriously.

OLIVER. You do? Why?

MOORE. I can make things very difficult for you.

ROBERT. Mr. Moore, we are used to dealing with white people who are a good deal more difficult that you could ever be.

MOORE. I don't appreciate being compared to your government.

ROBERT. Then stop acting like them.

*(***OLIVER** *rushes between them.)*

OLIVER. Robert, that was not a nice thing to say.

ROBERT. That's why I said it.

OLIVER. You should apologize at once.

ROBERT. No.

OLIVER. *(smiles)* Okay.

MOORE. You're all being incredibly irresponsible about this. You can't go on living in your own little world, you know.

OLIVER. We can try.

MOORE. Well, it won't work.

(He picks up his briefcase, starts to leave.)

ROBERT. We are not the irresponsible ones, Mr. Moore. We are not a group of misguided American whites walking into the middle of a fight we do not understand.

*(**MOORE** stops.)*

MOORE. Why do you keep referring to the fact that I'm white?

ROBERT. I couldn't help noticing.

*(**OLIVER** laughs)*

MOORE. I'd like to think the color of my skin doesn't make any difference.

ROBERT. I'd like to think that too.

MOORE. And that it doesn't disqualify me from being allowed to care about your people – from trying to do something to help them. You may not be able to appreciate that, but some do.

ROBERT. Really?

MOORE. Yes. It so happens we have the support of several black organizations.

ROBERT. Do you?

MOORE. Yes.

ROBERT. All Americans, I suppose.

TYLER. I doubt it very much, Robert. I've never even heard of this group.

MOORE. Perhaps you've heard of the South African National Council.

*(**OLIVER** looks at **ROBERT**.)*

TYLER. Maybe they've turned against you.

ROBERT. Impossible.

TYLER. How can you be so sure?

ROBERT. Because of who they are – what they stand for.

OLIVER. My foolish friend here has unshakable faith in the council. It comes from going to prison for them when they were banned by the government.

TYLER. You're a member?

ROBERT. I was. I joined when I was a boy. But I haven't been a member for a long time. Nine years.

OLIVER. *(smiles)* Not since he met me.

ROBERT. Not since I left prison.

TYLER. *(impressed)* How long were you in prison?

ROBERT. That was along time ago. It's over. You have to go on with your life – try to forget about it.

TYLER. Can you do that?

ROBERT. You have to try.

(There is an awkward silence.)

OLIVER. I was in prison too, you know.

TYLER. You?

OLIVER. That's where we met.

TYLER. I didn't know that.

OLIVER. Oh, yes. Robert and I are both very dangerous men.

TYLER. *(laughs)* Really?

OLIVER. Oh, yes. Extremely.

ROBERT. Oliver was only there toward the end. Short-time.

OLIVER. My crime may not have been as glamorous as yours, but it was a serious offense, and I will not allow you to belittle it.

ROBERT. Why don't you tell him what you were arrested for?

OLIVER. What does that matter?

ROBERT. Tell him, Oliver.

OLIVER. *(proudly)* I was judged to be a threat to national security.

ROBERT. Oliver –

OLIVER. Well, of a sort.

ROBERT. He was arrested for public drunkenness and indecent exposure.

*(***TYLER*** laughs.)*

OLIVER. A clear case of governmental oppression.

ROBERT. He got drunk and took his trousers off in the street.

OLIVER. *(correcting* **ROBERT***)* Not just my trousers!

ROBERT. And he was seen by two white girls driving by.

OLIVER. Those girls shouldn't have been in that neighborhood anyway. But of course I was the one who ended up in trouble. They had to go and tell the police all about the crazy kaffir they had seen.

ROBERT. The "crazy kaffir" – yes. That is what Oliver was called in prison – even by our own people.

OLIVER. I used to recite Shakespeare in my cell at night. *(Recites)* "O, that this too too solid flesh would melt" – and slide out between the bars!

TYLER. You must've been a big hit.

ROBERT. Oh, he was. He had a captive audience – me. They put us in the same cell for a time as part of my punishment.

OLIVER. I don't remember you complaining. *(To* **TYLER***)* If anything, he encouraged me.

ROBERT. Actually, having Oliver there made it almost tolerable. *(To* **OLIVER***)* Almost. *(To* **TYLER***)*
I knew nothing about the theatre before we met. After my release, I found him and convinced him we should start our own theatre group.

OLIVER. Yes, well, we all make mistakes.

ROBERT. Oh, has it been so bad? We just finished this play in London. We are finally in America. After this we go to New York. *(Pause)* We have come a long way.

OLIVER. *(sincerely)* That's true.

ROBERT. Farther than I every thought we could.

OLIVER. *(leans close)* Yes, well, you've never had much of an imagination.

ROBERT. *Ja?*

OLIVER. *Ja.*

> (**ROBERT** *tries to hit him.* **OLIVER** *screams and runs.* **TONY** *enters hurriedly through the house.*)

TONY. *(calling)* John! John!

TYLER. *(laughing)* What's the matter?

TONY. We've got a problem!

TYLER. What?

TONY. There're people outside!

OLIVER. Already? Customers? My multitude of adoring fans?

TONY. No, *demonstrators!*

TYLER. Oh crap.

TONY. With signs and everything! What are we going to do?

TYLER. How many of them are there?

TONY. I don't know, I guess about a dozen.

TYLER. *(relieved)* He made it sound like a lot more than that.

TONY. But they're blocking the front doors!

TYLER. They are?

TONY. Yes, and the side one too.

TYLER. I don't believe this.

> *(He rushes offstage, toward the back of the house. Stops.)*

That man from before –

TONY. Mr. Moore?

TYLER. Is he out there?

TONY. I didn't see him. These people just came up the street all of a sudden. What do you want me to do?

TYLER. I don't know.

TONY. We've got to do something.

TYLER. Did they try to get in?

TONY. No.

TYLER. Well, you better lock the doors anyway.

TONY. I already did.

TYLER. Good. Okay, stay by the doors. Keep them all locked. If they try to get in, or if Moore shows up, you let me know.

TONY. Okay.

(He runs out the back of the house.)

TYLER. And be careful! *(To* **ROBERT** *and* **OLIVER***)* Well, he's made good on his threat. I can't believe this is happening here.

OLIVER. *(suddenly subdued)* Why should here be different than anywhere else?

ROBERT. How much trouble can they give us?

TYLER. I'm not sure. He's right about the publicity. It might very well scare some of our audience away.

ROBERT. But not all of them.

TYLER. Who knows? It will if things get out of hand, and there's real trouble.

ROBERT. Is that likely to happen?

TYLER. I don't know. It sounds like they've got something other than just a protest in mind if they're blocking the doors.

ROBERT. You mean your people?

TYLER. Yes, the rest of the cast and the crew. He saw they weren't here. He must be thinking this will increase the pressure.

ROBERT. You think they'll try to keep them out?

TYLER. It looks like it. *(Thinks)* Can you go on tonight without a final run-through?

ROBERT. Of course. But if they won't let your people in they won't let the audience in anyway.

TYLER. You're right.

*(**TONY** runs in again from somewhere in the house.)*

TONY. John? That guy Moore showed up.

TYLER. Does he want to come in?

TONY. No. He said to ask you if you're ready now to cancel the production.

TYLER. I'd better talk to him.

TONY. You can't.

TYLER. Why not?

TONY. He's gone.

TYLER. Gone? Where'd he go?

TONY. He said you should call him at his coalition's office with your answer.

(He runs back out.)

TYLER. I'd better call the police first.

ROBERT. No, don't. Not yet.

TYLER. I don't want to either, but what else can we do?

OLIVER. I think we should ignore them.

ROBERT. This is no time for jokes, Oliver.

OLIVER. I'm not joking. If we refuse to deal with them, they will get discouraged and go away.

TYLER. Don't you believe it. They wouldn't be doing what they're doing if they were willing to just leave without getting what they want.

ROBERT. *(to **OLIVER**)* He's right.

OLIVER. Then we should call the police at once.

ROBERT. We can't do that.

OLIVER. Why not? We can have them beaten and jailed and be done with them.

TYLER. The police won't do that.

OLIVER. Well, they should.

ROBERT. I don't believe I'm hearing this. You want to call the police in on demonstrators? Haven't you seen enough of that?

OLIVER. As long as we have the power on our side for once, let's use it.

ROBERT. No, Oliver.

OLIVER. Well, what do you want, Robert? What do you suggest we do?

ROBERT. We should wait.

OLIVER. Wait? For what? For the idiots of the world to come to their senses? *(***ROBERT** *says nothing.)* Robert, our papers are temporary. After New York we must go home. Until when? When will they let us out again?

ROBERT. We'll get out again. What are you talking about? What's that got to do with this?

OLIVER. All that time in London – free of having to carry a passbook, free of curfew and finally, finally, finally knowing we weren't being watched by the security police. *(Pause)* And all that time ahead of us in New York. I want to do this play in New York. I just want to be free long enough for that! Is that so much to ask?

ROBERT. No, Oliver.

OLIVER. If it is, we may as well go back now.

TYLER. Don't talk like that. You're still in America – you're still free.

OLIVER. *(wheeling on* **TYLER***)* Am I free now?

TYLER. Well, these people outside aren't exactly security police.

OLIVER. Police, demonstrators, whatever – they're all the same. They're all *politicians.* They all use politics to get what they want and to hell with anyone who gets in their way.

ROBERT. Oliver –

OLIVER. These people will stop us.

ROBERT. No, they won't. I meant what I said – we'll do our performance on the street if we have to.

OLIVER. I know we're in trouble when you begin to believe your own rhetoric.

TYLER. Please, please, don't worry. If we keep our heads, we'll work this out.

OLIVER. You think so? I've been dealing with the politicians all my life, and it never works out for people like us. They have the power, so we have to beg them to let us do anything – everything – even what we were put here to do.

ROBERT. We have never begged.

OLIVER. And the power is all that matters to them. Who has it? Who can hold onto it? Who can take it away? It's a game to them, a game they play with our lives. And what do we do? We let them!

ROBERT. It's not that we let them, Oliver. What can we do to stop them?

*(**TONY** rushes in from the back of the house.)*

TONY. John!

TYLER. Yes?

TONY. There's someone else now who wants to come in.

TYLER. Someone else – not Moore?

TONY. No, a woman.

ROBERT. *(startled)* An *African* woman?

TONY. I don't know. I think so.

OLIVER. You see? It's true.

ROBERT. It can't be.

OLIVER. It is.

ROBERT. It *can't* be.

TONY. What should I do?

*(**TYLER** looks at **ROBERT**.)*

ROBERT. Let her in, please.

OLIVER. *(protesting)* No!

ROBERT. Yes – we have to. *(To **TYLER**)* Please.

TYLER. Go ahead, Tony.

(**TONY** *exits through the back of the house.*)

OLIVER. We're making a terrible mistake.

ROBERT. What are we supposed to do – not talk to her?

OLIVER. That's right.

ROBERT. We have got to let her explain. I want her to explain *this*.

TYLER. Should I call the police?

OLIVER. Yes!

ROBERT. *(to* **TYLER***)* No. *(To* **OLIVER***)* No!

TYLER. Would you rather speak to her alone?

ROBERT. No, no, you stay – you're part of this. Let her say what she has to say out loud to all of us.

(**EMILY NGOME** *enters through the back of the house.* **TONY** *follows her in. She stops just before reaching the stage.* **TONY** *hangs back.*)

EMILY. Gentlemen. Good afternoon.

ROBERT. *(disbelieving)* Emily – ?

EMILY. Robert. Oliver. It is good to see you both again. *(To* **TYLER***)* You must be Mr. Tyler, the festival director.

TYLER. Yes, I am.

EMILY. *(bows slightly, great dignity)* I am Emily Ngome.

TYLER. How do you do? *(He gestures toward* **ROBERT** *and* **OLIVER**.*)* I take it you know –

EMILY. We are old friends. Robert and my husband were very close.

ROBERT. *(to* **TYLER***)* Emily's husband was Peter Ngome. He was chairman of the council when I was a member.

EMILY. When the council was banned by the government, they were arrested together.

TYLER. Is he out, too?

ROBERT. He was released three years after me. But he was arrested again later and died in police custody.

TYLER. Oh – I'm sorry.

EMILY. Thank you. But please do not be embarrassed to speak of it. We must speak of it.

ROBERT. *(after a pause)* John, can you give us a minute?

TYLER. Oh. Sure. Tony, let's check the doors.

*(He exits with **TONY**.)*

EMILY. *(to both of them, in Xhosa)* Kunjani?

*(**OLIVER** turns away, does not reply.)*

ROBERT. Andiva – How did you get here?

EMILY. What do you mean?

ROBERT. Out of the country?

EMILY. The usual way for us.

ROBERT. Us?

EMILY. The council underground.

ROBERT. You're working with the council?

EMILY. I am now, Robert.

ROBERT. Since when?

EMILY. Some months ago.

ROBERT. But Emily, that's too dangerous. They watch you continuously. (**EMILY** *shrugs.*) How can you do anything for the council?

EMILY. I can only operate outside the country. I am living in Lusaka now.

ROBERT. You left home for good?

EMILY. Not for good. For now.

ROBERT. I didn't know.

EMILY. You have been out of touch, Robert. You have been busy. Traveling the world. Acting.

*(**TYLER** returns.)*

TYLER. I'm sorry, but you should know. Our people have started to arrive.

ROBERT. What's happening?

TYLER. They're across the street – waiting. So they don't confront the demonstrators.

ROBERT. Emily, what's going on? How can you be protesting our production?

EMILY. We are not.

OLIVER. Your lackey, Mr. Moore, claims you are.

EMILY. Mr. Moore is not our lackey. He is our ally.

ROBERT. We thought *we* were your allies.

EMILY. We hope that you are.

ROBERT. What's that supposed to mean? Haven't we always been?

EMILY. Then you will help us.

ROBERT. Do what?

EMILY. Help us face this crisis.

ROBERT. We don't know anything about a crisis.

OLIVER. Except the one we're in the middle of.

EMILY. Ten days ago, one of our people was murdered in Paris. The evidence indicates he may have been killed by agents of the Bureau of State Security.

ROBERT. The government has begun killing council members in other countries?

EMILY. We believe so.

ROBERT. That could be disastrous.

EMILY. Precisely. *(To* **TYLER***)* We have offices all over the world, with hundreds of members who have operated in the open for years. Our government never interfered because they never dared to. But now they have. They have escalated the conflict. And if they continue, it could mean a bloodbath.

ROBERT. Has everyone been ordered into hiding?

EMILY. Of course.

ROBERT. Even so – even if the government doesn't intend any more killings, they've managed to disrupt your operations for a while.

EMILY. We do not believe that is all they intend. We must respond. We must call attention to the incident, create as much public outcry as possible, to demonstrate to the government that they cannot do such things without consequences. We must stop this new reign of terror before it begins.

OLIVER. And what has this got to do with us?

EMILY. It was decided to ask you to cancel your production here as an act of protest over the murder.

OLIVER. You know we can't do that. You know what will happen if we do.

ROBERT. I don't understand. It was decided to *ask* us? Then why weren't we asked? Why didn't you come to us yourself?

EMILY. I only just arrived. I had to go first to our office in Washington.

ROBERT. So instead you sent some white American –

OLIVER. – lackey –

ROBERT. – to talk us?

EMILY. No.

TYLER. No, that can't be. This murder was ten days ago? Mr. Moore first called me three *weeks* ago. He must've decided to protest your production before this murder even took place.

ROBERT. Emily, what's going on?

EMILY. That is true. Mr. Moore informed us he intended to protest your production – before he contacted Mr. Tyler.

ROBERT. He asked for your support?

EMILY. Yes.

ROBERT. And what did the council say?

EMILY. We saw no reason for your appearance here to be protested. We told him that.

ROBERT. Then why does he think the council is supporting him?

EMILY. Because, when I arrived in America, I asked for his help.

ROBERT. You?

EMILY. Yes.

ROBERT. You told him to stage a demonstration against us?

EMILY. No, I did not authorize that.

ROBERT. But you sent him to talk to us –

EMILY. No. You do not understand, Robert. I did not send Mr. Moore to speak to you – I sent him to speak to Mr. Tyler. I asked him to convince Mr. Tyler to cancel your production, without involving the two of you.

ROBERT. Why?

EMILY. So that you would not have to cancel yourselves.

ROBERT. But if that is what the council sent you to do –

EMILY. I thought if the decision was kept between Mr. Moore and Mr. Tyler – strictly between the Americans – then the government might not hold you responsible. In his announcement to the media, Mr. Moore would specify the murder as his reason for the protest.

ROBERT. Get us cancelled to protest a murder by the government? It doesn't make sense.

EMILY. It was the only way to get the media attention we need *and* to keep you two blameless. That is why I went to Washington – to send word of my plan back to the council through our office there. I am now waiting for their confirmation.

ROBERT. But this is not the council's plan.

EMILY. No, but I am certain they will agree to it.

OLIVER. Nothing is certain.

EMILY. *(to* **OLIVER***)* The council understands the position they are asking you to put yourselves in. They did not make the decision lightly.

OLIVER. But they made it.

ROBERT. Yes, they did not think of such a plan. Their first thought was to throw us to the lions.

OLIVER. Maybe not their first thought, but they got around to it.

EMILY. Do not judge them too harshly. They fear they may be fighting for their lives – and the life of our movement. *(To* **TYLER***)* You see now why it is so important you cooperate?

TYLER. I don't understand.

EMILY. You can still agree to Mr. Moore's request. We can all simply act as though Robert and Oliver and the council were not involved.

TYLER. I see.

EMILY. Well?

TYLER. Well, what? I don't want to cancel their production. And don't ask me to do it to help your council – that's not my priority.

EMILY. But if Robert and Oliver want you to?

TYLER. If they want me to, I'll – I'll figure something out.

ROBERT. What about the festival?

TYLER. Oh, it'll be a disaster – there's no question about that. Of course, so is this demonstration.

ROBERT. Emily, there's no guarantee your plan will do any good.

EMILY. But if it does any good at all?

ROBERT. I don't know. *(Pause)* Oliver?

OLIVER. What?

ROBERT. What do you think?

OLIVER. What do I think? I think no.

ROBERT. No?

OLIVER. They're playing games with our lives. I've had enough of it.

ROBERT. But, Oliver – it's the council.

OLIVER. I don't care! I don't care who it is, and neither will the government. You're all kidding yourselves. They won't care who cancels what.

EMILY. It is possible.

OLIVER. They've been waiting for years for us to get directly involved, and the minute we do they'll move against us!

EMILY. You have always been involved. Your plays have always made political statements.

OLIVER. On stage!

(He seizes the back curtain, closes it violently.)

In the theatre! *We* never said those things. Do you understand? If we made the same statements ourselves – publicly – if we cancel this production, or let it be cancelled – they'll use it as an excuse to charge us with "supporting a revolutionary organization." And you know the punishment for that. If we don't go to prison, at the very least we'll be banned.

TYLER. Banned? How do you ban a human being?

ROBERT. It's a legal action they use when they can't convict you of any particular crime. You are made to stay in one place of the government's choosing – sometimes hundreds of miles from your home. You can't work. You can't write anything, or be quoted by anyone. And you are forbidden from speaking to more than one person at a time except for members of your family.

TYLER. My God.

ROBERT. You cease to exist as a public person.

OLIVER. A fine fate for an *actor*.

TYLER. But at the trial you could prove I cancelled this production – not you.

ROBERT. There is no trial.

TYLER. No trial?

ROBERT. It's just an order that comes down from the government.

TYLER. You can't put up any defense?

ROBERT. No.

TYLER. How long does it last?

ROBERT. A ban? Years. Often they are not lifted at all.

TYLER. What do you mean? It could last the rest of your life?

EMILY. No – until the government falls

OLIVER. The rest of your life.

TYLER. How are you supposed to live?

OLIVER. Ah – now, that's a good question. Let's ask Mrs. Ngome. Peter was banned after they let him out of prison. How did Peter live?

EMILY. He – lived.

OLIVER. Did he? For how long? What happened to him?

EMILY. You know he refused to obey.

OLIVER. Yes? Go on.

EMILY. He would not be silenced. He continued to speak out.

OLIVER. Until – ? *(To* **TYLER***)* Until they killed him. "Resisting arrest."

EMILY. He did what his loyalty demanded, and we can all learn something from his example.

OLIVER. I agree – that's why I intend to perform tonight. I too refuse to be silenced – by anyone.

EMILY. It is not the same thing! Not at all – and you know it!

*(****MOORE*** *enters in a hurry from the back of the house. He carries a sealed envelope.)*

MOORE. Mrs. Ngome! A courier just brought this from the council office in Washington.

EMILY. Where is he?

MOORE. He left.

EMILY. He left? He did not wait for an answer?

MOORE. No.

*(****EMILY*** *opens the envelope, takes out a note, reads it silently.* **MOORE** *moves onto the playing area.)*

TYLER. I didn't realize something this serious was at stake, Robert. I have to agree with Oliver. You can't let them put you in that kind of danger.

ROBERT. I don't know.

TYLER. What little might be accomplished just isn't worth the risk.

ROBERT. It would end the demonstration.

TYLER. To hell with the demonstration. Let them do whatever they can – we'll deal with it.

ROBERT. I don't want to jeopardize your festival.

TYLER. And I don't want to jeopardize your lives. I don't want to be a part of anything that might do that.

EMILY. *(finished reading)* That does not matter, Mr. Tyler.

TYLER. What do you mean? Why not?

EMILY. You are no longer involved.

ROBERT. Why? What does it say?

EMILY. *(after a pause)* I am ordered to proceed as originally instructed.

ROBERT. They still want us to cancel on our own?

EMILY. Yes.

ROBERT. They don't agree with your plan?

EMILY. No.

ROBERT. Why not?

EMILY. They have their reasons.

ROBERT. What reasons?

EMILY. They are not important.

ROBERT. We have a right to know the reasons, Emily.

EMILY. The council feels – if you cancel the production yourselves – it will have more of an impact.

OLIVER. You see? Games!

ROBERT. I don't believe it.

OLIVER. I do!

ROBERT. Is that all we mean to them?

EMILY. No –

ROBERT. What then?

EMILY. You must understand their position, Robert –

ROBERT. *Their* position?

EMILY. Yes, they need –

ROBERT. What about ours? What about what may happen to us if we do what they want?

EMILY. They have considered that.

ROBERT. Oh, have they?

EMILY. Of course. And even though they do not want to, they must still ask for your help.

ROBERT. *(after a pause)* And even though we don't want to – we must refuse.

EMILY. You do not mean that, Robert.

ROBERT. Yes, I do.

EMILY. You cannot refuse them.

ROBERT. Yes, I can!

EMILY. No, you cannot. *(After a pause)* If you do – I am instructed to inform you – that if you go ahead with your production here, the council will order a boycott of your future productions at home.

ROBERT. What?

EMILY. And you know the people will obey.

ROBERT. Is that what the note says?

EMILY. Yes.

ROBERT. Let me see that.

(He moves toward her, reaches for the note.)

EMILY. Robert – no!

*(She steps back and behind **MOORE** to shield herself. **ROBERT** stops, face-to-face with **MOORE**, shocked by what she has done.)*

EMILY. *(cont.)* Don't you understand? You must do what they ask.

ROBERT. Ask?

EMILY. This is one battle they do not intend to lose.

ROBERT. Well, you can tell them they have lost it. The government has never been able to intimidate us – does the council think they can?

EMILY. They are not trying to intimidate you.

ROBERT. What do you call it?

EMILY. I call it a plea for help.

ROBERT. A plea?

EMILY. Our movement is at stake.

ROBERT. Whose movement? Yours!

EMILY. Ours. You know what the council means to us – to all of us.

ROBERT. Not to all of us – not anymore.

EMILY. Don't say that.

ROBERT. What do you expect me to say? The council was the only thing outside myself that for most of my life I could believe in. And now they do *this*?

EMILY. They are our only hope –

ROBERT. They were, yes – they were – When I was ten years old and got up with my father early every morning so I could look out the window and see him walking to work with all the other men – hundreds of men all walking down our street because they were boycotting the buses – That is what they were. That was hope. That is the organization I joined – not this.

EMILY. They are still that. Do not abandon them now.

ROBERT. They are abandoning us.

EMILY. And what of your loyalty? You took an oath.

ROBERT. Loyalty? Loyalty works both ways. Anything else is – obedience.

EMILY. Then – do not do if for the council. Do it for your people.

ROBERT. Who are my people?

EMILY. You know the answer to that, Robert. You know who you are. Who and what you have always been.

ROBERT. Do I?

EMILY. Yes.

ROBERT. No, no – I don't. Not anymore. *(Pause)* Yes. Yes, I do. I am an actor. An actor – that's all.

EMILY. Robert –

ROBERT. That's all I am.

EMILY. You are an actor, yes – but still South African, still black, still Xhosa.

ROBERT. No.

EMILY. Yes!

ROBERT. I am none of those things.

EMILY. You are. You are. You cannot change who you are.

ROBERT. Of course I can. That's what actors *do*.

EMILY. On your little stage. But what of the real world? What of your country?

ROBERT. My country?

EMILY. Yes, your country. What of your brothers?

ROBERT. *(stamping his feet on the stage)* This is my country – *this*. *(Points to* **OLIVER** *and* **TYLER***)* And these are my brothers. I am a part of nothing else.

EMILY. You cannot live only in the theatre, Robert. You are still involved, whether you like it or not.

(Silence)

OLIVER. *(to* **TYLER***)* If we perform here, the council will ruin us as actors at home. If we don't perform, the government will ban us, and we'll be ruined as well. Either way – *(to* **EMILY***)* – we are fucked.

TYLER. Wait a minute. There's got to be another answer. What if you emigrated – just left it all behind? Then they couldn't make you cancel. So what if they ruin things for you at home? You're got a career outside. You can work here in America, in Europe, anywhere. I'll help you all I can. Our board has friends in the theatre all over the world.

ROBERT. It's impossible. That's called taking an exit permit – where they let you out, but you can never go back.

TYLER. Well, why don't you do it?

ROBERT. We have always had the option, if we were willing to leave our home and our families behind.

TYLER. Couldn't we get them out somehow?

ROBERT. The government would never allow it.

OLIVER. Besides, from the sound of it – if we emigrated, I doubt very much the council would let us defy them and go unpunished. They have friends all over the world too, and they would make our lives miserable. *(To* **MOORE***)* Isn't that right, Mr. Moore?

MOORE. I wouldn't do that.

OLIVER. Oh, wouldn't you?

MOORE. No. Believe it or not, I've been trying to do the right thing.

OLIVER. What difference does that make?

ROBERT. *(after a pause)* Then that's it, isn't it? Either way, we are finished.

EMILY. Then I can tell the council you will do what they want?

ROBERT. *(unbelieving)* That is what you want to know? I say we are ruined, and *that* is what you want to know?

EMILY. I tried, Robert. I did try.

OLIVER. "I tried." And I thought *I* was the one who said meaningless shit.

*(***EMILY*** is furious, but before she can speak* **ROBERT** *does.)*

ROBERT. No.

EMILY. No – what?

ROBERT. How can we do what they want? If we cancel, and the government bans us, how will we work? I don't mean as actors – as anything? How will we support our families? What about Oliver and Lisa and all their little ones? How will he feed them, and everything else? And what about my parents? You know they depend on me. You know my father can't work anymore. How am I supposed to care for him and my mother? It's not just us – you know?

EMILY. I know.

ROBERT. If we go ahead and perform, and the council punishes us – ruins us as actors at home – at least we will not be banned. At least we will be able to work – at something. We can care for our families.

EMILY. That cannot be your final answer.

ROBERT. Yes, it can. It is. You tell the council – they ask too much.

EMILY. I will not do that.

ROBERT. Then tell them whatever you want! I don't care. But tonight Oliver Manzi and Robert Obosa are going to be on this stage.

EMILY. Robert, no. You do not understand. If you defy the council –

ROBERT. What?

EMILY. You will force them –

ROBERT. We are not forcing anyone to do anything.

EMILY. *(after a pause)* If I am unable to convince you to cooperate – my instructions are – *(She glances at the note she is holding, as though even she cannot believe what it says.)* To advise you that the council disavows any responsibility for the consequences of your decision.

ROBERT. What consequences?

EMILY. There may be consequences.

ROBERT. A boycott of our productions at home. We understand that. What else are you saying?

EMILY. That the council does not want you to suffer for your decision, but they will not be held responsible.

ROBERT. For what?

EMILY. For what may happen.

ROBERT. And what is that?

EMILY. They may not be able to control the people.

ROBERT. The council has always controlled the people

EMILY. They may not be able to now. There may be – reprisals.

ROBERT. *(stunned)* Are you threatening us?

EMILY. You may be placing yourselves in danger.

ROBERT. Emily –

EMILY. And – your families.

OLIVER. You are threatening our families?!

*(He charges toward **EMILY**. **ROBERT** blocks his way, stops him, throws him back. During the following, **OLIVER** moves dejectedly across the stage and sits on the floor beside the road box, leans against it.)*

EMILY. I did not say that. You may be.

ROBERT. We'd be in no danger unless the council ordered it!

TYLER. This is extortion. *(He starts to leave the stage.)* We don't have to listen to this!

ROBERT. John, wait!

TYLER. No – this time I'm calling the police!

ROBERT. They can do nothing. What can they do?

TYLER. I don't know –

ROBERT. You will only make it worse.

TYLER. I've got to do something. I can't watch this and not do something!

ROBERT. There is nothing you can do. Please.

TYLER. *(after a pause)* All right.

ROBERT. *(almost pleading)* Emily, they can't do this.

EMILY. They have not done anything.

ROBERT. Don't play games with us! Not with us!

EMILY. I am not playing a game.

ROBERT. You can't be part of this.

EMILY. I have no choice.

ROBERT. Of course you do. You always have a choice.

EMILY. No.

ROBERT. Yes!

EMILY. I made my decision, Robert. I made it when I joined the council.

ROBERT. You made the decision to destroy your friends?

EMILY. No –

ROBERT. Because that is what you are doing. You want to destroy the government – fine, of course, we all do. But don't destroy us – and don't destroy yourself.

EMILY. I made the decision to serve the people – to help them –

ROBERT. How can this help our people?

EMILY. And to do it through the council. They are our only hope – you know that.

ROBERT. But they're trying to use us, Emily – and they're using you, too. Why do you think they sent you to talk to us, not someone else? Why do you think they sent a friend – ?

EMILY. I know that. It doesn't matter.

ROBERT. It does matter.

EMILY. They needed something done. Why shouldn't they use any means at their disposal?

ROBERT. Because it's wrong.

EMILY. Whether it's right or wrong does not matter, Robert.

ROBERT. You know you don't believe that. You tried to help us – with your plan.

EMILY. And I was wrong to do that. I should have followed my instructions. *(Almost crumbles the note in her hand)* That's been made clear.

ROBERT. You thought you had a better way to achieve the same goal – tell them that.

EMILY. I did.

ROBERT. Tell them again.

EMILY. No!

ROBERT. Try!

EMILY. *(softly)* No.

ROBERT. Emily, think of what you are doing!

EMILY. Things must be done, Robert. Things we do not want to do, but we must do.

ROBERT. What about Peter?

EMILY. Don't talk to me about Peter.

ROBERT. Would he have done this? If Peter were alive – would he allow this?

EMILY. That is irrelevant.

ROBERT. Would he?

EMILY. He would have made whatever sacrifice was necessary.

ROBERT. Yes, *he* would have – but he would have never asked it of someone else. And he would have never betrayed his own people!

EMILY. You claim you are not one of our people, remember?

ROBERT. You know what I mean.

EMILY. And you are not in the council anymore!

ROBERT. So I am expendable? So Oliver and I and our families are to be sacrificed?

EMILY. Just don't accuse us of betrayal, Robert. You are the one who left the council.

ROBERT. I left the council – all right, yes. Do you know why? Did Peter ever tell you why?

*(***EMILY** *begins to speak, stops herself.)*

When Peter was finally released, Oliver and I were performing in Johannesburg. Peter came to see us. We met in secret. He told me they wanted him to take an exit permit, but he wouldn't. He was going to stay in the country so he could rebuild the council, this time underground. But he knew he was about to be banned. I told him I wanted to help, but he said, no – I was known, I was being watched, it was too dangerous for me and it could jeopardize his work. I should stay away. But if I wanted to help, I should keep on performing. He had seen our play, and its effect on our people, and he saw some whites were starting to break the law to come to our performances. And he thought I was making as much of a contribution as I could doing what I was doing. And he gave us his blessing. *(Pause)* I didn't leave anything, Emily. *(Pause)* He never told you about that, did he?

EMILY. *(hurt)* I am sure there are many things Peter never told me. But that does not matter, Robert. That has nothing to do with now. Now you are either with us or against us.

ROBERT. Peter didn't believe that. None of us did.

EMILY. Perhaps if he had, the council would not still be fighting!

ROBERT. So the answer is to become inhuman? To betray your friends? Because that is what you are doing.

EMILY. After thirty years of oppression and sacrifice and lost lives and suffering – who dares call us inhuman?

ROBERT. After thirty years of oppression and sacrifice – I do.

EMILY. Very well, then we will be inhuman. That will be our sacrifice. But for it we will win our freedom, and our children's freedom. You can have your moral superiority, Robert. We will have our victory. And history will not remember us for having been inhuman. It will remember us for having won. *(Pause)* I must have your answer.

OLIVER. Can you possibly not know what it will be? What choice have you left us? Do you think we might still perform, knowing what you will do to the people we love?

ROBERT. No, Oliver. No. It's still up to us, no matter what she does. You remember I told you – my last year in prison, after they let you out, most of the time I was alone? Well, once, for a while, I had a man with me. I never knew who he was. He couldn't tell me his name because when they first threw him into my cell his jaw was already so badly broken he couldn't speak. And it never healed. They made sure they beat him often enough so it wouldn't. *(Pause)* One night – after his beating – they brought him back to our cell and I listened in the dark while he died. It took most of the night. In the morning, when they brought that shit they fed us, I ate his, too. When they came for him again, to beat him, I dared them – take me instead! They were happy to oblige. They were bored with beating him. *(Pause)* I kept them from finding out for a few days. I even dragged his body around the cell so that when they looked in they would think he had been moving. But, then he started to smell, and – They thought I had gone crazy when I refused to give him up. They stood in the door with their guns on me, cursing, shouting their lungs out – faces all red. I just pulled him with me back against the wall and waited for them to shoot. *(Pause)* And nothing happened. *(Pause)* I started to laugh at them standing there watching me holding this dead man in my arms. And I realized, the thing was – they were waiting, waiting for me, waiting to see what *I* would do. I still had choices, Oliver. Even then. I could come to my senses, be a good kaffir, say – "Ja baas" – and give him up. Or I could hold onto him until they came in and beat me. Or – I could walk straight into their guns. Whatever happened, it would be because of the choice *I* made. Whatever they did would be in reaction to *me*. They were no more free than I was. They were as bound by me as I by them because we were men in confrontation. They could limit my choices, but they could never eliminate them. Because I was still a human being. And this was something all their laws

– and prisons – and guns – and power – could not take away from me, could never take away – from me!

OLIVER. She still has the power, Robert.

ROBERT. No, Oliver. Not now. Not at this moment. At this moment – she is nothing. She has made her threats. She has done all that she can do. Now, she must wait – wait for us to decide what *we* will do. And right now – until we decide – and show her what she can do – she has no power over us – WE ARE FREE MEN!

EMILY. *(after a long pause)* You cannot still perform, Robert.

ROBERT. Yes, we can.

EMILY. Defy the council?

ROBERT. Yes.

EMILY. And sacrifice your families?

ROBERT. And sacrifice our families! We *can*!

EMILY. But you will not.

(She starts to leave the stage, stops, looks back at **ROBERT.** *He says nothing. To* **MOORE.***)*

EMILY. *(cont.)* Come.

*(***EMILY*** leaves the stage, exits through the back of the house.)*

ROBERT. *(after a pause)* Mr. Moore? Did you want something else?

MOORE. I didn't want – no.

(He leaves the stage, exits after **EMILY.***)*

ROBERT. *(to* **TYLER***)* John, thank you for all of your help.

TYLER. I wish there was something I could do.

ROBERT. You did all that you could. As much as anyone could ask.

TYLER. Thank you for that.

ROBERT. We're sorry about the trouble. For the festival, I mean.

TYLER. We'll deal with it – somehow. You're going to stay a while aren't you?

ROBERT. I don't think so.

(**TONY** *enters from the back of the house.*)

TONY. The protesters are leaving.

TYLER. Yes, it's over.

TONY. Should I tell our people it's okay to come in?

ROBERT. We'd rather not see anyone, if you don't mind. No need for them now anyway.

TYLER. I understand. I'll send them home. Excuse me, I've got a lot to do –

(*He begins to leave,* **ROBERT** *stops him, puts out his hand,* **TYLER** *takes it in both his hands.*)

ROBERT. Thank you.

TYLER. Come on, Tony.

(**TYLER** *leaves the stage, exits through the back of the house.* **TONY** *follows him out.* **ROBERT** *moves over near* **OLIVER**.)

ROBERT. Oliver, are you all right?

OLIVER. (*After a pause*) Have you ever wondered, my friend, in all these years – how different things would've been if they couldn't touch us?

ROBERT. What do you mean?

OLIVER. If we'd given ourselves over wholly to our art. If we were without wives, or children –

ROBERT. Without parents?

OLIVER. Yes.

ROBERT. Without homes?

OLIVER. Then they could not get at us.

ROBERT. They would get at us – through our friends.

OLIVER. If we were without connection to this world at all – if we lived only on stage – then we would be free.

ROBERT. Then they would round up our audiences, and without them our freedom would be meaningless.

OLIVER. No – it wouldn't.

ROBERT. Who would we act for?

OLIVER. We would act for each other – as we did in prison.

ROBERT. Ah – then, they would kill one of us. *(Pause)* It's a beautiful thought, Oliver, but it's got nothing to do with this real world.

OLIVER. That's why it is a beautiful thought.

ROBERT. *(after a pause)* Let's go.

(He opens the road box, takes out **VLADIMIR***'s hat, looks at it.* **OLIVER** *stands, moves toward the tree, stands looking at it.)*

OLIVER. You know, Robert – we should have taken that final exit permit a long time ago.

*(***ROBERT** *looks at him, gets an idea, turns back, lets the top of the road box close with a slam. He gets up on it, puts on the hat, unties the cord holding up his baggy trousers, lets them fall down around his ankles. He holds out the cord toward* **OLIVER.***)*

OLIVER. *(cont.)* Don't try to make me laugh.

ROBERT. Would I do that?

OLIVER. Well, if we're going, we'd better change our clothes.

ROBERT. Why?

OLIVER. Why?

ROBERT. Yes, why?

OLIVER. Isn't it obvious?

(He gestures toward his costume.)

ROBERT. This is the way I am going home.

(He gets down off the road box, moves toward **OLIVER** *by the tree, clumsily, because all the while his trousers are down.)*

OLIVER. It is.

ROBERT. Yes.

OLIVER. Like that.

ROBERT. Yes.

OLIVER. Well, you don't want to be arrested for indecent exposure, do you? At least pull on your trousers.

ROBERT. *(smiles)* What?

OLIVER. Pull – *(He realizes what **ROBERT** is doing.)* on your trousers.

ROBERT. You want me to pull off my trousers?

OLIVER. *(yells)* PULL ON YOUR TROUSERS!

ROBERT. True, true.

(He quickly pulls up his trousers, belts them with the cord.)

OLIVER. You're very childish – you know that?

ROBERT. I?

OLIVER. Yes.

ROBERT. More than you?

OLIVER. Much more than me.

ROBERT. Ah – are you certain?

OLIVER. *(after a pause)* Nothing is certain.

ROBERT. Nothing is certain?

OLIVER. No.

ROBERT. That's terrible. Are you certain?

OLIVER. *(smiles)* Yes.

ROBERT. Ah – that's reassuring.

(They both laugh a little.)

OLIVER. *(after a pause)* Well? Shall we go?

ROBERT. Yes, let's go.

(They do not move. The lights slowly fade to black.)

End of Play

www.ingramcontent.com/pod-product-compliance
Lightning Source LLC
Chambersburg PA
CBHW071414290426
44108CB00014B/1820